SEISMOSAURUS

THE LONGEST DINOSAUR

by

Elizabeth J. Sandell

DINOSAUR DISCOVERY ERA

Bancroft-Sage Publishing

601 Elkcam Circle, Suite C-7, Box 355, Marco, FL 33969

Exclusive distributor

Britannica

ENCYCLOPAEDIA BRITANNICA EDUCATIONAL CORPORATION

TRAINING & DEVELOPMENT

310 South Michigan Avenue Chicago, IL 60604

LIBRARY OF CONGRESS CATALOGING IN PUBLICATION DATA

Sandell, Elizabeth J.
  Seismosaurus: the longest dinosaur

  (Dinosaur discovery era)
  SUMMARY: Describes the discovery of fossilized remains of the
longest dinosaur yet known, what has been learned so far from the
remains, and what we currently believe about the dinosaurs in
general.
  1. Seismosaurus--Juvenile literature. (1. Seismosaurus. 2.
Dinosaurs. 3. Paleontology) I. Oelerich, Marjorie L. II. Schroeder,
Howard. III. Vista III Design. IV. Title. V. Series.
QE862.S3S358   1988   567.9'7   88-963
ISBN 0-944280-03-X (lib. bdg.)
ISBN 0-944280-09-9 (pbk. bdg.)

International Standard Book Number:	**Library of Congress Catalog Card Number:**
Library Binding 0-944280-03-X	88-963
Paperback Binding 0-944280-09-9	

SPECIAL THANKS FOR THEIR HELP AND COOPERATION TO:

David D. Gillette, Ph.D., Curator of Paleontology, New Mexico
Museum of Natural History, Albuquerque, New Mexico
and
Mary R. Carman, Paleontology Collection Manager
Field Museum of Natural History, Chicago, Illinois

SEISMOSAURUS

THE LONGEST DINOSAUR

AUTHOR

Elizabeth J. Sandell

dedicated with love to Leila Fellner Oelerich Mumma

EDITED BY

Marjorie L. Oelerich, Ph.D.
Professor of Early Childhood and Elementary Education
Mankato State University

Howard Schroeder, Ph.D.
Professor of Reading and Language Arts
Dept. of Curriculum and Instruction
Mankato State University
Mankato, MN

ILLUSTRATED BY

Vista III Design

BANCROFT-SAGE PUBLISHING
112 Marshall St., Box 1968, Mankato, MN 56001-1968 U.S.A.

INTRODUCTION: DISCOVERING SEISMOSAURUS

"This footprint must be from the biggest animal ever found!" exclaimed Mai Lee.

Mai Lee was looking at a plastic copy of a great big footprint. Dr. Sanford, a paleontologist, had brought it in a suitcase to show to the class. Paleontologists study fossils. Fossils are parts of plants and animals that lived many years ago. Their remains were buried in rock and soil. The footprint Dr. Sanford showed the class was about 24 inches (61 cm) across.

"Mai Lee, what do you mean by the word 'biggest?'" Dr. Sanford asked.

"I mean the animal that weighed the most, was the tallest, and was the longest!" Mai Lee answered excitedly.

"The largest animal alive today is the blue whale, which lives in the ocean," Dr. Sanford said. "It weighs 100 to 130 tons (90 to 117 metric tons). It is also about 98 feet (30 m) long.

"Some dinosaurs were almost as big as a blue whale," Dr. Sanford continued. "These dinosaurs were very big animals that lived thousands of years ago. The word 'dinosaur' means 'terrible lizard.' These animals were given this name because they were very big. Scientists used to think that they must have looked like lizards."

CHAPTER 1: FOSSIL CLUES

Scientists know about dinosaurs from fossils which are found in layers of rock. When a dinosaur died near water, its body might have been covered with mud. The water containing hard minerals would wash through every hole in the dinosaur's bones. Then the minerals would turn the bones into fossils.

HUGE BONES WERE FOUND

In 1979, a music teacher found fossil bones from the very longest dinosaur ever known. Arthur Loy from Albuquerque, New Mexico (USA), was walking in the desert. He stopped at the edge of a cliff to look into a valley. As he walked away, Mr. Loy saw some big bones sticking out of the rocks.

Dr. David Gillette, curator of paleontology at the New Mexico Museum of Natural History, heard Mr. Loy's story. On Father's Day weekend in 1985, Dr. Gillette went camping in the desert. He and his family camped where Mr. Loy found the bones. Dr. Gillette's daughter, Jennifer, helped find the large fossil bones. Jennifer was only thirteen years old, but she was very interested in fossils.

"That was the best Father's Day present anyone could get!" Dr. Gillette said after they found the fossils.

Scientists are working very carefully to dig out more fossil bones. While they dig, they use a jackhammer and chisels to remove the rocks so they can get to the bones. Workers have found bones from the tail, ribs, and legs of this dinosaur.

EARTH SHAKER LIZARD

Dr. Gillette named this big dinosaur *Seismosaurus* (siz´ muh sor´ uhs). This word means "earth shaker lizard." *Seismosaurus* might have been 100 feet (30 m) long and weighed 80 to 100 tons (72 to 90 metric tons). Dr. Gillette thinks it might have been about 18 feet (5.5 m) high at its shoulders.

"We still have much more than the tail, ribs, and legs to dig up," said Dr. Gillette. "We hope to find a whole skeleton. It takes a long time to dig the bones out of the rock."

Until more is known about *Seismosaurus,* we can learn how it might have lived by studying other large dinosaurs that ate only plants.

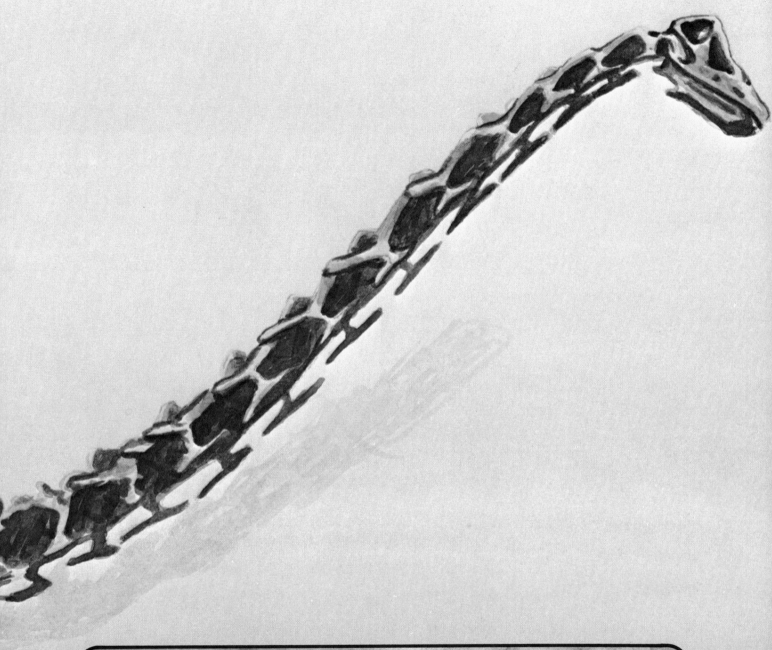

27 ft
24 ft
21 ft
18 ft
15 ft
12 ft
9 ft
6 ft
3 ft
0 ft
Height

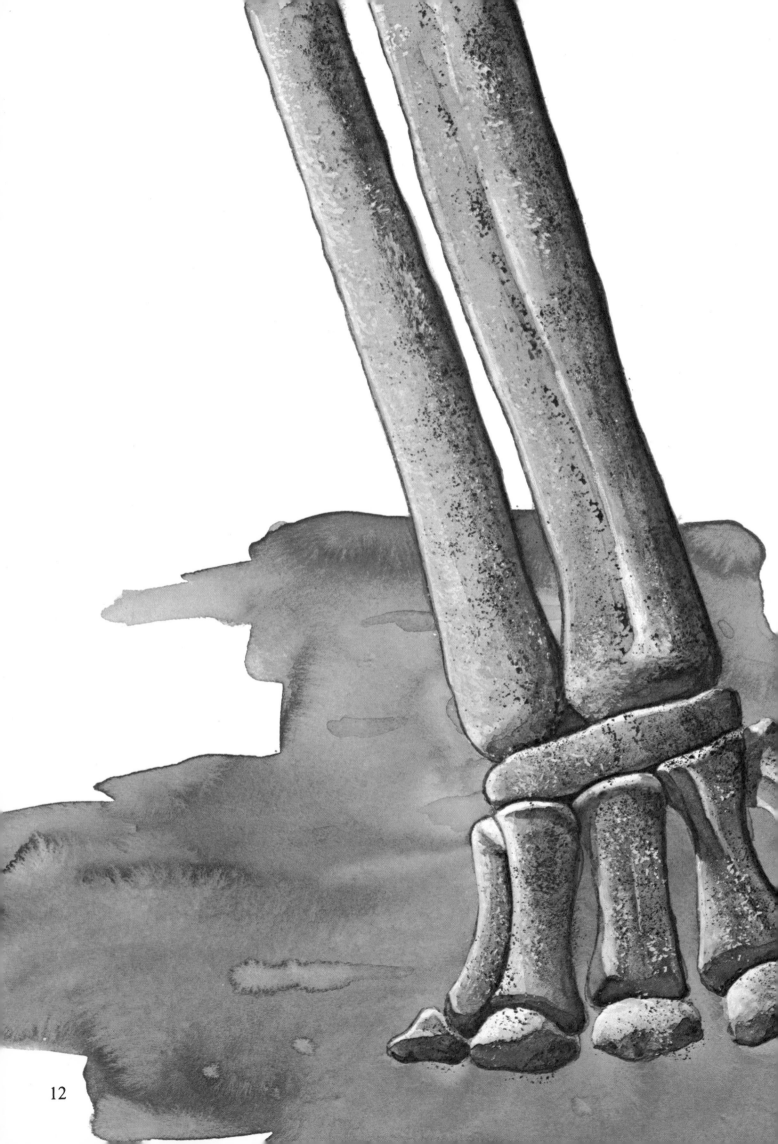

CHAPTER 2: SAUROPODS

The group name for these big dinosaurs is *sauropod* (sor´ uh pod). The Greek word **sauros** for "lizard" was put together with the word **pod** for "foot." The feet of these dinosaurs were like lizard feet, with five toes on each foot.

These *sauropods* walked on all four legs, which were like those of elephants.

They had big bodies, small heads, long necks, and long tails. Nose openings were high on their heads.

Sauropods probably laid eggs in nests.

TWO KINDS OF SAUROPODS

There were two kinds of *sauropods*. One kind had two front legs which were longer than the two rear legs. They had very heavy bodies, and long necks, like giraffes.

Brachiosaurus (brak´ e uh sor´ uhs) and *Ultrasaurus* (ul´ truh sor´ uhs) were in this group.

Brachiosaurus may have been 75 to 91 feet (23 to 28 m) long. This dinosaur may have weighed 85 to 112 tons (76 to 101 metric tons).

Ultrasaurus was about 100 feet (30 m) long and weighed about 150 tons (135 metric tons).

The second kind of *sauropod* had four legs that were all the same length and they had very long bodies. *Apatosaurus* (uh pot´ uh sor´ uhs), *Diplodocus* (duh plod´ uh kuhs), and *Seismosaurus* were in this group. *Apatosaurus* is also known as *Brontosaurus* (bron´ tuh sor´ uhs).

Apatosaurus was 65 to 80 feet (20 to 24 m) long and weighed 30 to 35 tons (27 to 32 metric tons).

Diplodocus would have been 85 to 92 feet (26 to 28 m) long and weighed almost 12 tons (10.8 metric tons).

Seismosaurus was the longest of all the *sauropods*.

Seismosaurus

WORLD TRAVELERS

Fossils of *sauropods* have been found in many different countries.

When *Seismosaurus* lived on earth, there were many shallow seas.

The weather may have been very mild. There may have been warm, wet summers and no cold winters. *Seismosaurus* lived and roamed through the swamps, forests, and plains.

Earthquakes and volcanoes caused the land to shake and move up and down. Some land became mountains. Other land became the bottom of rivers.

Some of the rock where dinosaur fossils were buried was pushed to the top. That is the reason the big bones of *Seismosaurus* were near the cliff, where Mr. Loy saw them.

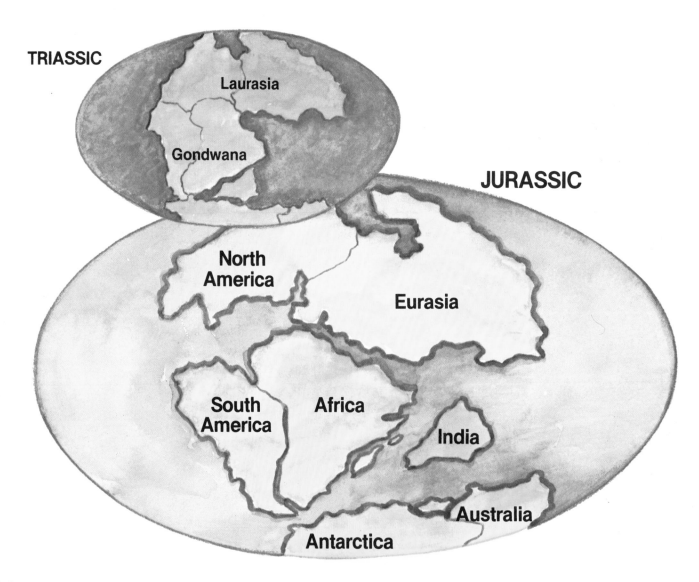

TRACKWAYS

Scientists used to think that these giant dinosaurs spent their time in lakes with their heads above water. Now, scientists believe that the *sauropods* would not have been able to breathe while in a lake. The weight of the water would have kept them from breathing.

Scientists believe that these dinosaurs traveled in groups. Many sets of footprints, called trackways, have been found together in small areas. The footprints were left when dinosaurs

walked together in swamps.

Smaller footprints of younger animals were found in the middle of the group. Here they were safe from enemies.

Trackways do not show tail marks. Scientists think the *sauropods* did not drag their tails.

Scientists can study the trackways to learn how fast the dinosaurs traveled. They believe that the *sauropods* went about 4 to 5 miles (6 to 8 km) per hour.

PEACEFUL PLANT-EATERS

These big *sauropods* ate only plants. With their very long necks, they could reach the tops of tall trees to eat leaves. They could eat other plants, too. These include horsetails, cycads, and vines that grew around tree trunks.

Fossils show that the *sauropods* had teeth in the front of their jaws but no teeth on the sides of the jaws. Some *sauropods* had teeth which were shaped like pencils. Some had spoon-shaped teeth. This might mean that the teeth were used for tearing off leaves and twigs but not for chewing.

Scientists believe that *sauropods* swallowed rough stones, called gastroliths. The stones rubbed on the food in their stomachs to help them digest the food, just like chickens do today. The stones would have worn smooth. Scientists have found thousands of smooth stones about 1 to 4 inches (2.5 to 10 cm) long near dinosaur fossils.

Since the *sauropods* ate only plants, there was no need for them to attack other animals for food. The fact that the *sauropods* were so big helped to keep them safe from enemies that might have attacked them. Smaller animals would not bother them.

The tough skin protected the *sauropods*. In addition, the big animals could use their long tails to strike out at any possible enemies. Also, adult *sauropods* could stand on their back legs to stomp on the attacker with their front legs.

Enemies like *Allosaurus* (al´ uh sor´ uhs) and *Ceratosaurus* (ser´ uh tuh sor´ uhs) were meat-eating dinosaurs. They might not have attacked a whole group of *sauropods*. Instead, they would wait for a dinosaur that was old, sick, or very young.

SMART THINGS TO DO

Scientists used to believe that the size of an animal's brain showed how smart it was. Now they know this is not always true.

Scientists now think that the way animals live is a better measure of how smart they are. Although dinosaur brains may have been as small as a cat's brain, there is other evidence to show that the dinosaurs were very smart.

Sauropods took care of their young and themselves, they traveled in groups, and they lived for many years. These were clever things to do.

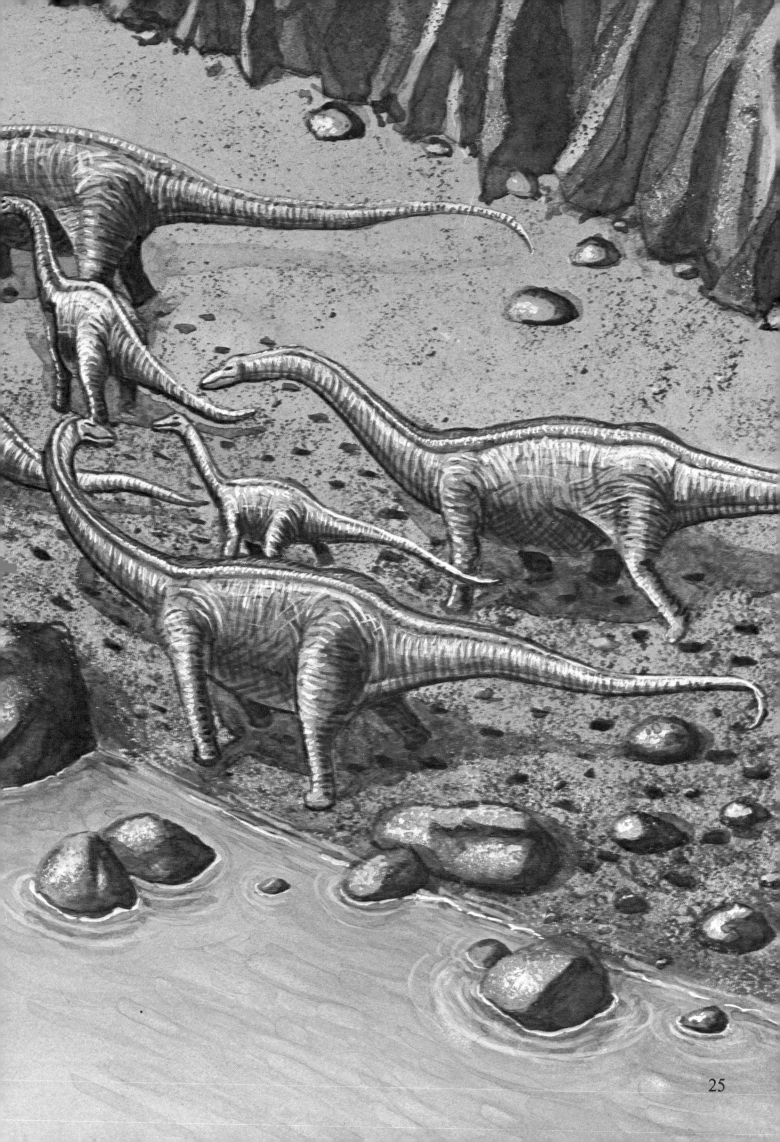

CHAPTER 3: NO MORE SAUROPODS

Scientists do not know how many years a dinosaur lived. Fossils show some might have lived as long as 120 years. Many scientists believe that dinosaurs kept growing as long as they lived. This would explain why they grew to be so big.

Scientists are not sure how the dinosaurs all died. Here are a few of the ideas.

1. The air cooled, and dinosaurs could not keep warm.
2. Meat-eating dinosaurs slowly killed the plant-eaters and then died from hunger.
3. Disease caused them to get sick.
4. Water flooded the earth.
5. A lump of rock about six miles (10 km) across crashed into the earth from space. This caused a cloud of dust that changed the weather.

Maybe none of these ideas is correct. No one really knows for sure why all the dinosaurs left. It may have taken thousands of years, but all the dinosaurs are gone.

CONCLUSION: STILL MORE TO LEARN

"When scientists make new discoveries, they change their ideas," Dr. Sanford told the class.

"Some scientists, like Dr. Gillette, think the important question is how dinosaurs lived, rather than how they died," Dr. Sanford continued. "Dr. Gillette and his team are still finding more of the fossils of *Seismosaurus*. This may help us in the future to learn more about how the dinosaurs lived."

MUSEUMS

Now we can see dinosaurs only in museums. Here are some places where we can see the fossils of sauropods.

American Museum of Natural History, New York, NY.

Brigham Young University, Provo, UT.

Carnegie Museum of Natural History, Pittsburgh, PA.

Denver Museum of Natural History, Denver, CO.

Dinosaur National Monument, Jensen, UT.

Duquesne University, Pittsburgh, PA.

Field Museum of Natural History, Chicago, IL.

Houston Museum of Natural Science, Houston, TX.

National Museum of Natural History, Smithsonian Institution, Washington, DC.

New Mexico Museum of Natural History, Albuquerque, NM.

Peabody Museum of Natural History, Yale University, New Haven, CT.

Utah Natural History State Museum, Vernal, UT.

W.H. Reed Museum, Laramie, WY.

GLOSSARY:

ALLOSAURUS (al´ uh sor´ uhs) means "other lizard" or "different lizard." The Greek word **allos** means "different," and the word **sauros** means "lizard." The backbone of Allosaurus was different from that of all other dinosaurs.

APATOSAURUS (uh pot´ uh sor´ uhs) was a big plant-eating dinosaur. It is also called "Brontosaurus." Apatosaurus is from the Greek word **apatelos** which means "deceptive" and the word **sauros** which means "lizard."

BRACHIOSAURUS (brak´ e uh sor´ uhs) means "arm lizard," because its front legs were longer than its back legs.

BRONTOSAURUS (bron´ tuh sor´ uhs) means "thunder lizard." It is from the Greek word **bronte** which means "thunder" and the word **sauros** which means "lizard." This dinosaur is now known as Apatosaurus.

CERATOSAURUS (ser´ uh tuh sor´ uhs) means "horned lizard" from the Greek words **keratos** for "horned" and **sauros** for "lizard." It had a horn on its nose, a big head, saber-like teeth, bony knobs over its eyes, and short legs. It ate only meat. It walked on two hind legs.

CURATOR (kyoo ra´ tuhr) is a person in charge of a museum or other place where things are collected.

CYCAD (si´ kad) is a fern-like tree which lived many years ago.

DINOSAUR (di´ nuh sor´) means "terrible lizard." The Greek word **deinos** means "terrible," and the word **sauros** means "lizard."

DIPLODOCUS (duh plod´ uh kuhs) means "double beam," because it had "Y"-shaped spines on its tail bones. The Greek word **diplos** means "double," and **dokos** means "beam."

FOSSILS (fos´ uhlz) are the remains of plants and animals that lived many years ago. The Latin word **fossilis** means "something dug up."

GASTROLITH (gas´ truh lith´) is a small rough stone swallowed by animals to help them digest their food. The stones rubbed on the food in their stomachs. Thousands of smooth stones about four inches (10 cm) long have been found near dinosaur fossils. The stones would have worn smooth from rubbing together in the stomach.

LIZARD (liz´ uhrd) is a kind of reptile. Most lizards are small with slender, scaly bodies; long tails; and four legs.

MUSEUM (myoo ze´ uhm) is a place for keeping and exhibiting works of nature and art, scientific objects, and other items.

PALEONTOLOGIST (pa´ le on tol´ uh jist) is a person who studies fossils to learn about plants and animals from thousands of years ago. The Greek word **palaios** means "ancient," **onta** means "living things," and **logos** means "talking about."

SAUROPOD (sor´ uh pod) is the family name for the large, plant-eating dinosaurs. It is from the Greek words **sauros** for "lizard" and **pod** for "foot."

SCIENTIST (si´ uhn tist) is a person who studies objects or events.

SEISMOSAURUS (siz´ muh sor´ uhs) is the longest dinosaur ever found. The word is from the Greek **seismos** for "earthquake" and **sauros** for "lizard."

SKELETON (skel´ uh tuhn) is the framework of bones of a body.

THOUSAND (thou´ zuhnd) is ten times one hundred. It is shown as 1,000.

TRACKWAYS (trak´ waz) are paths which are well worn from the feet of passers.

ULTRASAURUS (ul´ truh sor´ uhs) is a large sauropod that was about 100 feet (30 m) long from head to tail. It probably weighed about 80 to 100 tons (72 to 90 metric tons). The name is from the Latin words **ultra** for "beyond" and **saurus** for "lizard."

TIME LINE

PERIOD	CHARACTERISTIC ANIMAL LIFE
CRETACEOUS 65 MILLION YEARS TO 135 MILLION YEARS AGO	Triceratops, Pteranodon, Corythosaurus, Tyrannosaurus rex, Plesiosaurus, Tylosaurus
JURASSIC 136 MILLION YEARS TO 192 MILLION YEARS AGO	Brachiosaurus, Allosaurus, Stegosaurus, Dimorphodon, Camptosaurus, Seismosaurus
TRIASSIC 193 MILLION YEARS TO 224 MILLION YEARS AGO	Mastodonsaurus, Rutiodon, Protosuchus, Plateosaurus
PERMIAN 225 MILLION YEARS TO 279 MILLION YEARS AGO	Eryops, Seymouria, Dimetrodon, Titanophoneus
CARBONIFEROUS 280 MILLION YEARS TO 345 MILLION YEARS AGO	Urocordylus, Hylonomus, Branchiosaurus

AGE OF THE DINOSAURS